2007
A POETRY ODYSSEY

After a voyage of 2,500 years, poetry has finally reached the stars ...

West Midlands
Edited by Mark Richardson

 Young**Writers**

First published in Great Britain in 2007 by:
Young Writers
Remus House
Coltsfoot Drive
Peterborough
PE2 9JX
Telephone: 01733 890066
Website: www.youngwriters.co.uk

SB ISBN 978-1 84602 856 4

Foreword

This year, the Young Writers' *2007: A Poetry Odyssey* competition proudly presents a showcase of the best poetic talent selected from thousands of up-and-coming writers nationwide.

Young Writers was established in 1991 to promote the reading and writing of poetry within schools and to the young of today. Our books nurture and inspire confidence in the ability of young writers and provide a snapshot of poems written in schools and at home by budding poets of the future.

The thought, effort, imagination and hard work put into each poem impressed us all and the task of selecting poems was a difficult but nevertheless enjoyable experience.

We hope you are as pleased as we are with the final selection and that you and your family continue to be entertained with *2007: A Poetry Odyssey West Midlands* for many years to come.

Contents

Ashlawn School, Rugby

Eleanor Bowes (11)	1
Bethany Woodings (11)	2
Bethan Baldwin (11)	3
Niamh Gold (11)	4
Georgia Wood (11)	5
Hannah Summers (11)	6
Robert Lloyd (11)	7
Rikesh Lad (12)	8
Liam Smout (11)	9
Holly Vincent (11)	10
David Wilding (11)	11
Alexandra Ferguson (12)	12
Charlie Randle (11)	13
William Meadowcroft (11)	14
Gregory Lyttle (11)	15
Thomas Curtis (11)	16
Sián McKechnie (11)	17
Kiera Boughey (11)	18
Eve Holden (12)	19
Talha Qaisar (13)	20
Daniel Roberts (13)	21
Sanjeev Singh-Dhillon (13)	22
Francis Cafearo (13)	23
Lee Hughes (13)	24
Lyndon Mapplethorpe (13)	25
Ami Cranton (13)	26
Eloise Lucas (11) & Shannon	27
Conlan Morrow (11)	28
Danielle Lawson-Kirby (11)	29
Jamie Morgans & Jevan Khalsa (11)	30
Hannah Wright (13)	31
James Robinson	32
Hannah Sharpe (13)	33
Sarah Rollins (14)	34
Claire Nellis	35
Paige Makepeace (13)	36
Charly Malins (14)	37
William Ratcliffe	38

Aqib Farooq (13)	39
Holly Godfrey (14)	40
Luke Mason (15)	41
Mark Thomas (15)	42
Andrew Oldroyd (15)	43
Nicole Hutchinson (15)	44
Alexander Teasdale (12)	45
Sophie Evans	46
Bertie McLaren (11)	47
Maya Mistry (11)	48
Hannah Maltby (12)	49
Alex Jones (12)	50
Courtney Rees (12)	51
Ryan Evans (12)	52
Peter Bernard (12)	53
Fabian Joyce (12)	54
Rebecca Dandy (12)	55
Damini Mistry (12)	56
Edward Andrew (12)	57
Beth Duffin (12)	58
Harriet Davies (12)	59
Sam Green (12)	60
Grace Marsella (12)	61
Amy Wadsworth (12)	62
Laura Barratt (13)	63
Laura Dunn (12)	64
Abbey Grocott (12)	65
Jack Cannell (12)	66
Kyle Batchelor (13)	67
Rebecca Goodyer (13)	68
Alex Bolland (13)	69
Natasha Bourne (12)	70
Mayuri Patel (12)	71
Jay Francis-Wint (12)	72
Kat Cooney (12)	73
Fiona Betts (13)	74
Katie Braithwaite (14)	75
Luke Horrocks (14)	76
Izzy McLaren (13)	77
Louis-Philippe Delaugere (12)	78
Viresh Mistry (14)	79
Chloe Williams (13)	80

Gene Parker-Brombley (13)	81
Elliott Youds (13)	82
Ella Slatcher (13)	83
Joe Fenwick-Wilson	84
Alice Stewardson (11)	85
George Walshe	86
Frances Elliott (12)	87
Laura Maybury (11)	88
Kati Simpson (11)	89
Shaun Stuart (11)	90
Olivia Kelly (11)	91
Thomas Swinford (11)	92
Helena Crisford (12)	93
Amanvir Nagra (11)	94
Lydia Iliff (13)	95
Katie Irwin (13)	96
Maddie Riddell (13)	97
Jordan Evans (13)	98
Shaun Boulter (13)	99
Shehzaad Mullah (13)	100
Josh Hammond (13)	101
Zainab Mogul (14)	102
Helen Gibson (13)	103
Melanie Johnson (15)	104
Grant Spooner-Roberts (15)	105
Katie King (11)	106
Kiran Dhariwal (11)	107
Ben Hollis (12)	108
Sonny Griffiths-Lynch (11)	109
Ryan Sabin (11)	110
Scott Crisp (11)	111
Liam Reynolds (11)	112
Daniel Francis (11)	113
Beth Lawrence (11)	114
Terry Morgans (11)	115
Nikesh Patel (11)	116
Alex Kerr (15)	117
David Morgan (15)	118
Aaron Stonard (15)	119
Tom Curley (15)	120
Amy Morris (13)	121
Samantha Clarke (13)	122

Leslie Clarke (12)	123
Ryan Welburn (12)	124
Reuben Desouza (11)	125
Robert Barnett (11)	126
Nicole Gulliver (11)	127
Vishan Parmar (11)	128
Denise Bladon (11)	129
Alexandra Lawton (11)	130
Matthew Threadgold (11)	131
Scarlett John (11)	132
Evangeline Wheeler-Jones (11)	133
Eleanor Garside (11)	134
Chloe Bell (11)	135
Harley Childs (11)	136
Mollie Brind (11)	137
Bethany-Jade Stratford (11)	138
Aaron Mills (12)	139
Hannah Swinford (11)	140
Kishan Vaghela (11)	141
Lewis Cutts (11)	142
Ellie Collins (11)	143
Jessica Edkins (11)	144
Sam Tuckey (15)	145
George Clark (11)	146
Lloyd Briggs (11)	147
Sam Colledge (11)	148
Akshay Vaghela (11)	149
Dilan Mistry (11)	150
Emily Dixon (11)	151
Anisa Patel (11)	152
Joe Beasley (12)	153
Felicity Webb (16)	154
Chris Givelin (15)	155
Jessica Holton (15)	156
Melissa Manani (15)	157
Danielle Wills (15)	158
Chéy Kirby (15)	159
Sarah Hirons (15)	160
Richard Lines (15)	161
Michael Hollowell (15)	162
Will Headley (16)	163
Eloise Barret (14)	164

Emily Waugh (13)   165
Tarot Aplin (13)   166
Chris James (13)   167
Jenny Thrower-Menzies (12)   168
Thomas Allman (12)   169
Thomas Wood (12)   170
Inderveer Uppal (12)   171
Amber Collings (12)   172
Brodie Neville (12)   173
Elizabeth MacLeod (12)   174
Niall Neeson (12)   175
Danielle Parker (12)   176
Arianna McKechnie (13)   177
Moneeb Razaq (12)   178
William Fulthorpe (12)   179
Becky Turtle (13)   180
Megan Ryan-Smith (11)   181

King Edward's School, Birmingham
Charles Whitehouse (11)   182

Round Oak School, Leamington Spa
Naomi Faria (15)   184
Dale Austin (13)   185

The Poems

Bully

It started in Year 4,
And now I'm in Year 6.
I did have friends, I'm sure of it.
It'd be my dream to be a happy kid.
You follow me to school,
You follow me back home,
Trying to annoy me,
But I just want you to go!
You ruined my party,
But that wasn't it,
If you asked me for money or lunch
And you didn't get it,
I might have been hit.
Was it jealousy because you maybe don't have much?
Should I hate you or should I feel sorry for you?
Maybe even like you a touch!
We don't have to be friends,
But I hate being foes.
Stop being a bully and leave me *alone!*

Eleanor Bowes (11)
Ashlawn School, Rugby

Bullying

If you are being bullied,
You can cry,
But tomorrow may come
As a punch in the eye.

The bully is the predator,
The victim is the prey,
We pray to God
That it will stop one day.

Kicking, punching, calling us names,
We don't want to be bullied,
And it is such a shame.

We fear to go to school,
Another day,
But . . .
The bully is the predator
And the victim is the prey.

Bethany Woodings (11)
Ashlawn School, Rugby

Hitting, Kicking, Calling Me Names

Hitting, kicking, calling me names!
My friends all ignoring me.
They are not really my friends, I just say that.
I say that so they don't get into trouble,
If they get into trouble they will beat me up.
At break time I just sit in the toilets.
If I go out they will hit me and beat me up.
They used to be my friends, we used to play together,
But now they are
Hitting, kicking, calling me names!

Bethan Baldwin (11)
Ashlawn School, Rugby

The Senses of Fear

I heard it again today,
The savage sound of harsh footsteps.
I froze, rooted to the ground,
Petrified as the footsteps gained on me.
The bitter taste of fear,
Like pins on the tip of my tongue.
The taste grew stronger and stronger,
As the footsteps grew louder and louder.
I closed my eyes,
Hoping that when I opened them again,
The world would no longer be against me.
I forced myself to hastily open one eye,
Only to see the clenched fists of the person
Who had made my life a misery.
Do I deserve to smell pain brewing in the pit of my stomach?
My life is like a shipwreck destroyed at the core.
I lost the will to be happy long ago,
All joy has been sucked from me.
Like a lemon,
Bitter and empty.
All I pray is that I can escape from this prison cell,
Escape from myself.

Niamh Gold (11)
Ashlawn School, Rugby

Wrong Or Right?

The last time I got an answer wrong was never.
That's why the bullies are here.
Around every corner and bend, they'll be there.
Look next time you're playing
Because I'll be bleeding and suffering.

Look at you and your friends . . .
Have you ever been a bully like them all?
Have you ever been bullied . . . like me?
Because you will know how it feels,
The bleeding, the suffering, the pain!

I have no will to live, my mother says there's light at the end
of the tunnel,

But there's none for me.
Will I survive one more day . . . ? Not so.

Georgia Wood (11)
Ashlawn School, Rugby

Bully

I can't believe you did that,
Leave my friend alone,
Give her back her hat,
You're a bully, I should have known.

Why are you doing this?
Now this time you've gone too far,
Oh my goodness,
You actually hit her with a metal bar.

Teacher, teacher, help!
She's bleeding, help her quick,
We need an ambulance now.
That boy he wanted a row.
My friend she's gone,
Never to be seen again.
An operation was done
But she was unlucky in the end.

Don't let bullies keep you down,
You are stronger than them!

Hannah Summers (11)
Ashlawn School, Rugby

Bullying Poem

Why do you make my life a misery?
What did I do to you?
I want an answer, I want it now,
You chase me forever it seems.
You make me upset and you give me bruises,
The bell for break brings fear to my heart.
I can't get food at lunch because my money is taken,
The last time I remember I had fun was . . .
I can't remember.
I constantly look over my shoulder,
I'm always scared to turn a corner.
My saviour is the home time bell.

Robert Lloyd (11)
Ashlawn School, Rugby

Trapped

Trapped in what seems a black hole
There is no way out
No one else except the bullies
Waiting for me
They rain misery upon me
I've been threatened time and time again
Hit many a time
I told my mum I lost my phone,
I didn't really,
They took it.
I didn't use it anyway
I don't have friends to call,
I go to the toilet and cry,
Floods of tears falling from my eyes.
My mother calls for me
Checking I'm alright.
She doesn't know I'm crying
I wipe my tears and say, 'I'll be out in a minute.'
I will try to make some friends
Socialise with others,
Stay with them throughout my life.
If I am unsuccessful in my hunt for friends
I have no other choice,
I shall suffer my fate through their actions,
They could waste my life!

Rikesh Lad (12)
Ashlawn School, Rugby

Anti-Bullying Poem

When another day arrives
Second by second feels like a year of despair
It's like the red hawk is hunting me down
Like a car has crashed off a bridge made of rubber
He thinks he's beat me;
But he hasn't and never will!

Liam Smout (11)
Ashlawn School, Rugby

Bullying

When I was bullied
Everyone teased me,
I had no friends,
Nobody sat with me at break or lunch.
No one to talk with, no one to play with.
I heard the bully approach me,
What could I do?
No one to turn to,
Nowhere to run to,
At that moment
All I could do
Was scream.

Holly Vincent (11)
Ashlawn School, Rugby

Bullying - Is it Right

The last time I had friends was year 1.
The last time I laughed . . . never.
I beg you, stop it . . .
I am sick with of rudeness,
The foul play of your unkindness,
Of the way you have treated me for the past six years.
Go now whilst you have the chance,
Whilst the wind blows you away.

David Wilding (11)
Ashlawn School, Rugby

I Used To Like School

I used to like school,
Every day was a joyous occasion,
But now I dread every moment of it,
The moment I reach the school gates,
The moment the school bell rings,
The moment lunchtime comes,
The moment I see her . . .

I just don't laugh anymore,
I just cry.
No longer do I have friends to support me,
I sit alone at break,
There may as well be no other children there,
To me the playground is a vast empty space,
Until she comes . . .

The last bell is music to my ears,
I walk, I see her, I run . . .
I arrive home, everything seems well until . . .
The phone rings, my sister answers, it's her . . .

A new day comes,
The same routine though,
Will I ever enjoy school again?

Alexandra Ferguson (12)
Ashlawn School, Rugby

Bullying

When I was coming out of my classroom,
Just going to the lunch hall,
These people from my year came up to me
And one of them nudged me so I dropped my lunch money
And the other one took my money
And then they both started to hit me
And I was shouting
Why do you always bully me?
Why are you doing it?
They wouldn't answer my questions,
Because by the time I had finished shouting at them
They had run away to the lunch hall to spend my money.
When I went to my friends the bullies came back,
But they couldn't take us all on
So they just walked by.
Now I always stick with my friends,
So when they walk by I just say, 'Goodbye'.

Charlie Randle (11)
Ashlawn School, Rugby

No Way Out!

Trapped, like a one-way street
Nowhere to go except backwards . . .
Into the pit of bullies.
I starve every day, no money for food,
Only blood from my own body.
I beg on my knees
Hoping for a snow day to come
So we get the day off.
But I guess even when we are off school . . .
I would still get bullied.
I have no freedom,
And I am stuck in my house,
Doomed if I step outside!

B ullying is the thing that is happening to me.
U nderachieving, too busy worrying about what will happen to me.
L ies which I have to tell my mum and teacher every day.
L aughing is something I've never done.
Y elling to tell them to *stop, please!*
I ndividual, always on my own.
N asty is what they always are to me.
G enerous is what they always are not.

William Meadowcroft (11)
Ashlawn School, Rugby

Stop Bullying

B is for bullying, coward at heart
U is for not understanding
L is for learning they can't control themselves
L is for laughing, that's all they do
Y is for you, stay big and strong
I is for ill, ill of mind
N is for nobody, just like me
G is for going now, I can't take this.

Stop bullying!

Gregory Lyttle (11)
Ashlawn School, Rugby

Bullying

I'm being bullied at my school,
I daren't fight back because,
They're bigger, fatter, heavier and stronger than me.
I want to run but they've got me surrounded,
I yell for help but my friend runs away,
Then he comes back with a teacher.
'Five weeks detention,' he says, 'it's a serious matter.'
I enjoy myself for the first time in a long time.

Thomas Curtis (11)
Ashlawn School, Rugby

Help Me!

B is for bullying
U is for you upset me
L is for you laughed at me
L is for lying here half-dead
Y is why did you pick me?
I is for I tried to ignore you
N is for you do nasty things
G is for *go away!*

Sián McKechnie (11)
Ashlawn School, Rugby

You Bully

The sight of my friend
the bitter taste from my mouth
the smell of torture
and somehow people still laugh . . .

Is it because of my race
even my hair
or my face?

I wonder what I should do
shall I tell you
my mum or my dad?
What have I done to you?

Are you jealous of poor little me
Why are you?
There is no need!

So leave me alone you bully
I won't take it
I'll stand by my friends . . .
that I haven't got
So you pick on someone else
You rot!

Kiera Boughey (11)
Ashlawn School, Rugby

Loyal Teddy Bear

Loyal teddy bear
I love your one glass eye
Oh how it makes me sigh
To know the truth of my little brave soldier
And how she was just left to smoulder.

Loyal teddy bear
I love your limp little paws
To know all the stuffing is on the floor
Oh how to know why that terrible deed was done
All for a little boy's fun.

Eve Holden (12)
Ashlawn School, Rugby

The Game

The weather was acting like ghosts were flooding the sky
as the players set out of the chilly changing rooms
The crowd roared like a pack of lions
The red shiny ball was thrown into the deserted sky
and landed on the slushy green grass
The bowler ran like the speed of light
The rain blistering his cold, numb face
his arm brushing his tomato-red ear
The wet ball smashing into the ground
bouncing off like a kangaroo
swiping all the rain in its path
The batsman stamped his knife-like studs into the dusty pitch
gripping his handle tightly
and slashing the bat into the path off the ball
the ball zooming like a supersonic jet into the roaring crowd
landed with a bang
destroying a plastic chair; into uneven pieces.

Talha Qaisar (13)
Ashlawn School, Rugby

The Race

On my motorbike at the starting gate,
The tension was rising, I could not wait,
From the left to the right were ferocious racers,
I hope to score big points like the LA Lakers.

The gate dropped and I let the clutch out,
My parents started to cheer and shout,
Shifting gears up and down,
I was riding my bike like a clown.
I put it into 4th gear,
I was jumping so high, I had no fear.

The second lap gone, I laid in 3rd,
My rival in front, his name's Chris Bird.
I turned too quick and was close to coming off,
The heat was rising as I went into the trough.
I caught up with the boy in second,
He was saving his position like Chris Kirkland,
The person in 1st was pulling away,
I could not let this happen because it was a girl called Fay.

I then went into second and started to ride in danger,
The steward was looking out carefully, like a red ranger.
I overtook Faye and it's the last lap!
I then went on to win the race,
I am a top chap!

Daniel Roberts (13)
Ashlawn School, Rugby

The Class

The class was on fire
Ablaze with light
Children everywhere, what a sight
It's nearly break, I can feel the earthquake
2 minutes left, I'm counting the seconds.

Break is here, I'm making the most
I suppose I can make myself some toast
5 minutes gone, I best savour the moment
Quiet, peace, peace and quiet
Oh no please, say it's not true
The hell is back, I need to go to the loo.

Sanjeev Singh-Dhillon (13)
Ashlawn School, Rugby

The Match

He strikes the ball with an iron foot
They think it is good but
What a save
That keeper's had a shave
It's a corner
Go McGorner
The cross comes in
You can hear a pin
Drop, it's an overhead kick
It's a little flick
It's in, it's a goal
There's the whistle
The winning crowd goes mad
The losers are sad.

Francis Cafearo (13)
Ashlawn School, Rugby

The Frog

The frog is slimy
Every time I go past it
I want to kick it
Its skin is grimy

It looks at me every day
It points at me with its big nail
It makes me go pale
It makes me run away

It hypnotises me with its eyes
It kisses me with its dirty lips
As I walk away it sways its hips
It tries to jump on your thighs.

Lee Hughes (13)
Ashlawn School, Rugby

The Cat

He moves like a shadow through the night
He makes the kill with awesome might

He swiftly devours his prey
He continues on his way

Through the night he roams
Quietly slipping past people's homes

He finds food where he can
He's a great annoyance to the binman

He skilfully kills the rats
Then madly chases after the bats

The animals lucky enough to fly
Know the only safe place is in the sky

Nobody knows from where he came
Nobody even knows his name

In the morning he slips away
To somewhere he can quietly stay.

Lyndon Mapplethorpe (13)
Ashlawn School, Rugby

The Scary Lion

T errifying teeth
H ates other animals
E ats everything he can find

S harp claws
C urly coat
A ngry look on his face
R eady to pounce
Y awns all the time

L ies in the desert all alone
I n amongst sand that he calls home
O ne by one he watches other animals go past
N ever not in trouble.

Ami Cranton (13)
Ashlawn School, Rugby

I Wish

They are waiting at the gate for me,
I try to run away,
I've got a pain in my tummy,
It happens every day.

The only friend I have is me,
I need someone to talk to and play games,
I want to go home again,
The place where it's safe and warm.

Oh my gosh, they're back again,
I wish I were never born,
I feel very small,
You never know,
This might be my last day at school.

Eloise Lucas (11) & Shannon
Ashlawn School, Rugby

Why Me?

Bullies will whisper till the bell has gone,
They will trap me, hit me non-stop,
I feel the punches getting harder.

What have I done to you?
Why am I treated so badly?
There's 6 of you and 1 of me,
Why, why, why?
Why do you do this?
Give me a chance,
So you can see there is nothing strange about me.

All of them are unpleasant
Thoughts and things stuck inside me
That will never go away,
Why, why, why?

Nobody will understand
That bullying causes so much harm,
I ask my mum *why*
You don't know how it feels.

Conlan Morrow (11)
Ashlawn School, Rugby

Bullies Big And Small

B is for *bullying!*
U is for upsetting!
L is for lying!
L is for laughing!
Y is for whimping!
S is for sadness!

B is for betrayal!
I is for intimidation!
G is for gangs!

A is for abuse!
N is for not nice!
D is for disastrous!

S is for scary!
M is for mean!
A is for amusement!
L is for large!
L is for life!

Danielle Lawson-Kirby (11)
Ashlawn School, Rugby

Bullying

Racism is bullying.
Please stop it now,
If you continue, you won't get very far.
If you ever feel you've been bullied,
Never feel guilty and keep it shut,
Just remember it's not your fault,
There are always jealous cowards in this world.

The last time I laughed
Was so long ago,
I can't remember.
I just stay and wait to witness pain
Again and again.
There's nothing about me,
I ask myself, 'Will this ever end?'
Sooner or later I'll break down and cry.
Let the darkness fill the room inside,
Like a bird cannot fly,
I'm lucky to have a family like mine.

Jamie Morgans & Jevan Khalsa (11)
Ashlawn School, Rugby

The Man-Eater

He looks at you with his big, round eyes
His eyes glare at you as he walks by.
His big, round feet or should I say paws,
Will pounce, painfully, using his long, sharp claws.

He's the king of the plains, the guard of his pride,
He pounces, playfully, like a wishy washy tide.

Hannah Wright (13)
Ashlawn School, Rugby

Bear

He protects the land
He knows like the back of his hand
The smell of rotting corpses
From the victims of his kills
The collective power he controls
Causes everything else to fall
He will always end up on top
When he takes the forest hops
He makes his way up to high ground
Where his mighty cave is found
He will glare upon the world
Other beasts below will curl
When he spots his prey and seals its fate
And then he sprints down to mutilate

James Robinson
Ashlawn School, Rugby

The Horrible Cat

He sits on the chair watching you.
Eyes are glowing green and blue.
His mouth is open ready to chew,
His teeth are sharp, his claws are too.

He follows and stares,
Screeches and glares,
He growls like bears,
And the pillowcase he tears.

You see him in the morning,
The afternoon and evening,
Staring at you with his eyes gleaming.

Hannah Sharpe (13)
Ashlawn School, Rugby

The Horrible Cat

He runs around the alleyways rummaging through the bins,
As I walk to work in the mornings
I see him licking dirty tins.

His fur is as hard as straw,
He has one wrinkly black paw.

I always seem to find his ginger fur
In bundles outside my back door,
This cat's health is poor.

Every night he sits
On the top of the washing line post
Like a king!

Sarah Rollins (14)
Ashlawn School, Rugby

Poem

I went to town to buy a book,
But somehow ended up in New Look.
I bought myself some brand new clothes,
When I went to the counter the girl raised her nose.
She stared at me and gave me evils,
And she moved away as if I had measles.
I paid for my clothes and got out of the shop
And went to buy some fizzy pop.
It made me hyper, I went mad,
And then went home, I was so glad.
I came home with bags of clothes
The bags were big, they overflowed.
I was so tired I went to bed,
And woke in the morning in a bedspread.

Claire Nellis
Ashlawn School, Rugby

The Killer Granny

I went to see my granny.
She ain't no ordinary granny,
She runs riot all day long.
There once was a burglar on the loose,
She said it wasn't her.
I went to see her the next day,
And she was in a cell.
She wears disco outfits and goes to lots of discos,
(She says she is going to bingo).
When I sleep at her house
I make sure I lock my bedroom door.
I make sure I have a bat;
To hit her with when she sleepwalks.
Be careful of my granny, she's a killer!

Paige Makepeace (13)
Ashlawn School, Rugby

Love

Love is adorable
Love is sweet
Love is for you and me
Everyone wants love - boys and girls
Everyone will get love - including you
And everyone will find their *true one!*

Charly Malins (14)
Ashlawn School, Rugby

Me, Me

As she sat next
   to me her voice
      caught attention
         to me even though
            her eyes blinded me
          and she made a
            plea, for me, my
               help, she wanted me.

               It's all about
              Me, me, me, me . . .

William Ratcliffe
Ashlawn School, Rugby

The Football Match

The referee blew his whistle for the teams,
And the players were very keen.
One goal was scored against Man U,
Then people started shouting when he blew the half-time whistle.
He blew the whistle and the crowd started shouting,
The manager saw the ball grasp the back of the net,
Another goal for Arsenal and the crowd goes wild,
The final whistle blows and it's 2-0 to Arsenal.

Aqib Farooq (13)
Ashlawn School, Rugby

Flying High

Flying high,
Flying high in the sky,
Looking back at what passes by,
The clouds shoot past,
So very fast,
I am slowing down, about to stop,
Just settled down on a rooftop,
Day by day people pass by,
Now do you know what I am?

Holly Godfrey (14)
Ashlawn School, Rugby

A New Season

A new season and everyone is ready to go.
Into the mud and dirt, into the bone-crunching hits.
Bodies on the line, everyone is ready to go.
New kit and equipment,
New players and crowds and everyone is ready to go.
The smell of the freshly cut grass
And freshly clean club, everyone is ready to go.
As the new season goes into the first game,
Everyone is ready to go.

Luke Mason (15)
Ashlawn School, Rugby

Watching You, Watching Me

I'm standing here watching you
In the bitter winter wind
The cold sun peeking over the horizon
You cast out into the blinding sun.

I watch you catch a fish
I am full of envy watching you
The wind bites once more
I'm now wishing I was home and warm.

I shiver in my winter boots
Watching you shake off the cold
I'm still here watching you
Learning as my luck has not changed.

Now the years have passed
I no longer feel the cold
I no longer envy you
And it is you now watching me.

Mark Thomas (15)
Ashlawn School, Rugby

Reality

Have you ever wanted something?
Something that you can't have?
A toy, a car, a house, a girl?
You work towards it. You pay towards it.
But you still can't have it.
There's always a reason.
Money, responsibility, practicality, personality.
After time you learn that there's no time for you.

You can try your best,
Your very hardest.
But in the end,
You realise it's not worth it.
But still you try and always will.
Because, still you hope,
That time will change it.
Though you know it won't.
Because that's not what happens,
In reality.

Andrew Oldroyd (15)
Ashlawn School, Rugby

Two Extra Shadows

From time to time
I look after my cousins
They may be fun
And make me smile.
But there's one thing
I feel as though
I have two extra shadows
Behind me.
They just want to feel older,
And want to feel grown-up.
It's nice they like to be like me,
But they can't see
It really bothers me.

I love them too much
So I won't get angry.
They are my beautiful cousins,
Who I will love forever.
Get mad, never!
I never shout
I just keep calm
And keep my cool.

Nicole Hutchinson (15)
Ashlawn School, Rugby

Circle Of Life

He is stalking the plains, preying on the weak
And his fiery coat burns all who look at it.

He is mocked by flashing lights and their clicking laughs
And his eyes are blinded by the nimbus beams.

He is old but also wise
And his brain is full of knowledge.

He is dying and will soon cease to be
And his family shall eat him and his son take the lead.

Alexander Teasdale (12)
Ashlawn School, Rugby

Interform Is Cancelled

The rain came,
Interform gone with the wind,
Everybody thought is was a shame,
And all disappointed within,
The rain was falling in buckets,
Hitting the windows hard.

Moaning and groaning,
As the teacher told the class,
That Interform was cancelled,
Disappointment was all around,
As the rain hit the ground
Splashing as it fell.

Thunder clashing,
Lightning flashing,
During lesson two,
As the memo came through,
Not a chance of things changing,
And not a thing to do.

Teachers had not planned anything,
As they thought it would be on,
So everybody's panicking now,
As Interform is out,
People who had bought their kits,
Were slightly annoyed.

Period three and period four,
What an utter bore,
As there will be lessons,
And Interform was no more,
Poor students feel so sad,
As the weather is so bad.

Nature's way has it,
That they can't do Interform today,
They will just sit in class,
Like every other day,
Hoping the rain will go away,
And they will do Interform another day.

Sophie Evans
Ashlawn School, Rugby

The Bully

I stand here on this tall building
And think of my past, but it will not last.
This is where I end, I will never mend.
When I jump I'll think of good things,
I think and think but I only have bad memories
Of when you torment me and crush my feelings.
I crouch down low and then I drop,
As I hit the ground it's just like you hitting me.
Goodbye!

Bertie McLaren (11)
Ashlawn School, Rugby

Bullying

He clenches his hand, ready to punch,
Blood trickles down my face,
He ceaselessly laughs at what he has done,
Then legs it at a fast pace.

He steals my lunch at dinner time,
He calls me a hurtful name,
If only it was the olden days,
Teachers could hit him with a cane.

Waiting for a reaction,
In front of his friends, he shows off,
They crowd around and cheer for him,
He suddenly strangles me, so I cough.

Tormenting me continuously,
Physical and mental abuse,
It's like I'm locked in jail,
I want to be let out, loose.

I haven't done anything to him,
Strong inside, is what I need to be,
It is pointless what he is doing,
I wish he would stop bullying me.

Every day, when I go home,
All I do is cry,
I'm not enjoying life at all,
All I can say now is bye.

Maya Mistry (11)
Ashlawn School, Rugby

Bullying Full Stop!

I am a tear,
I glisten in the light,
I was wept,
Sadness I portray.

I am blood,
I trickle down skin,
I was cut,
Hurt I portray.

I am a wrinkle,
I crease,
I am on a furrowed brow,
Anger I portray.

I am a person,
I bleed, I cry, I wrinkle,
And though you may not realise it,
I portray feelings.

Hannah Maltby (12)
Ashlawn School, Rugby

Why Is It You Bully Me?

Why is it you bully me? You make me so sad,
You make me feel so angry and very, very mad,
I can't play with anyone, you make me look like a Billy,
To me you are someone very, very silly,
Why is it you take my money?
Is it that your mates think it is funny?
I think you should stop,
But I know you will not,
You hurt me both sides,
Inside and outside,
I dread coming to school,
Because people think I'm a fool,
I know that you're not,
But, someone, make it stop!

Alex Jones (12)
Ashlawn School, Rugby

Pointless

It's pointless that people bully,
And make it all bad.
It's pointless they're vicious
And make the weaker feel sad.
It's pointless to waste time,
When they could be having fun,
It's pointless making people miserable,
So they see nor feel no sun.
It's pointless that they continue
Even when they are told off,
It's pointless that they could even start
Just over my stupid cough.

It's pointless that you're still here,
In front of me, terrifying me,
It's pointless you phone and text me too,
But how? I just don't see.
It's pointless you're still going, including your mates,
I'm going to leave now.
It's pointless to give my life away,
But I feel I have, so . . .
It's pointless you have made me kill myself,
But I guess you don't care, and I hope you're happy.

Courtney Rees (12)
Ashlawn School, Rugby

Odyssey To Sicily

On the calm, relaxed and azure sea,
A huge, gigantic ship set sail to thee.
The sailors had set off on an important odyssey,
To find the beautiful, ancient land of Sicily.

The crashing waves of the ocean lapped up against the ship,
The waves became reckless and its boards began to rip,
The sailors became frantic and worse was to occur,
It was to leave the sailors feeling like they had a hangover.

The sailors were hurled against the rocks,
They lay there, hurt and covered in knocks,
Some were killed, others survived,
With his ship the captain dived.

The sailors were never to finish their odyssey,
To find the beautiful, ancient land of *Sicily!*

Ryan Evans (12)
Ashlawn School, Rugby

Reading

Reading is a great thing,
No one ever dare fling
A book out of their way,
Otherwise I will have my say.

Books are a thing to read,
They fill you up with lots of greed,
To know what will happen next
In the story text.

Reading is for all ages,
But what most people do is just turn pages,
Not even looking at the text,
So they never know what to expect.

A book is like a friend,
Be very careful as you bend
The text-filled pages back,
Make sure everything is intact.

As now I conclude my speech,
I hope now teachers will teach,
The children of this text,
In this world you decide what happens next.

Now remember books are great,
So don't you ever hate,
Books at all for they are good,
So don't hide them under a hook.

So read them for your own interest,
So just remember that books are the best!

Peter Bernard (12)
Ashlawn School, Rugby

School Life

It can be good or it can be lame,
Overall it's just the same.
'Why do we need it?' many ask.
To get a job nice and fast.

Most of the teachers are really boring,
Set the students off snoring.
Due to that and a lack of attention,
Usually get yourself in detention.

Fabian Joyce (12)
Ashlawn School, Rugby

My Unhappy Garden

Outside of my window there's a little tree
And on that tree there is one leaf
There used to be a bee that visited that tree.

But as I watch intently, my gaze upon that bee,
I notice that one leaf, swaying unhappily
Wanting to be free from its misery.

Looking just below that tree, I notice a crowd,
That crowd is of daisies, chatting happily.
Then I hear a tiny cry, and spot another daisy standing all alone.

Outside of my window the grass is turning yellow.
The yellow grass is a mass of weeds
Set in a jungle.

You see, that's my garden,
It needs some TLC.
But with a little help
It will grow up steadily.

Well my little garden, in ways, is just like me,
So I hope this winter
My little tree with only one sad, little leaf,
And the one unhappy daisy,
And the yellow grass,
Will grow up and smile
So next year
I can tell a different *tale!*

Rebecca Dandy (12)
Ashlawn School, Rugby

Chocolate

Chocolate is great,
Chocolate is fun,
The reason it's cool,
Is that it fills up your tum.

Truffle and buttons,
Big fudge muffins,
Caramel is gooey,
Toffee is chewy.

I love brown Smarties,
They make me want to party,
I hate the coconut ones,
They make me want to run.

Dreams are like heaven
They're as white as a feather,
But the best are Twirls,
They make me want to swirl.

Overall they're nearly all great,
So hey, give me some *now!*

Damini Mistry (12)
Ashlawn School, Rugby

Shortbread Ship

Once I was on my shortbread ship,
Shortly we passed some mango dip.
Followed by a pea-green planet,
With a centre made out of granite.

A flock of floating sheep
Were in the universe deep.
The black forest gateaux came along,
It was defeated by a sausage called Billabong.

Then along came the sirloin steak,
So I ran at it with a rake,
'Prepare to die,'
Said the apple pie.

Now I'm dead
Covered in shortbread.

Edward Andrew (12)
Ashlawn School, Rugby

Sweet Shop!

I walk into the big, bright shop;
Colour is everywhere.
I look around with my taste buds tingling,
And all I can do is stare.

Strawberry, orange, lime and soda,
There are so many that I can see.
There's even an apple and blackcurrant flavour,
What more can there be?

Pink, yellow, orange, blue,
Many colours to look through,
There's those really, really sour sweets,
That make you mouth water loads.

I don't know which ones to buy,
There's so many to choose from,
But now my turn has come
To know which ones I want to buy,
And to share between me and you.

Beth Duffin (12)
Ashlawn School, Rugby

Sea Life

He swam;
Like a fish in water,
Over, under, over, under,
Down, down he went,
Surrounded by fish.
Orange, blue, yellow, green,
Every colour you could ever imagine.

Dolphin, dolphin,
He looked around,
Swimming towards him at the speed of light,
He grabbed a fin and was pulled along,
Jumping up and down, up and down,
Back down they went,
Letting go to see them swim away.

A noise;
Getting louder and louder by the second,
He saw it coming,
The size of many London buses,
The blue whale,
So calm and gentle,
But could kill in an instant.

Swimming back up,
But being pulled back down,
A constant fight with the current,
Not wanting to see him leave,
Swimming back up,
Getting there,
Breathing again,
Standing on the shore looking to where he had just been.

Harriet Davies (12)
Ashlawn School, Rugby

Burning

Burning brightly in the dark,
Nobody has noticed it is happening.
The crackling sound of burning,
Trees collapsing as it sweeps over the ground,
Animals of species flee to survive,
The fire swallows all in its path.

The fire dies down to a small flicker,
The sound of wailing, sirens fill the night air,
The fire is finished but will return
The forest is destroyed.
The fire may spark again but it is gone for now.

Sam Green (12)
Ashlawn School, Rugby

The Sweet Shop

The tall jars tower above us,
There's lots to choose from, the sweets go without fuss,
Jelly babies, Smarties and bonbons too,
Also plenty of chocolate for me and for you.

You go up to the counter with your money,
With a very large chocolate bunny,
You turn away and go out of the shop,
Walk home, get in, and turn the lock.

Then a girl comes with fear in her eyes,
'Have you got my bunny?' she cries,
'Yes, here's your rabbit, Mr Garrott,
Why don't you go and feed him a carrot?'

Grace Marsella (12)
Ashlawn School, Rugby

Rainbow Bridge

Come on boy, one last lick,
Before you're gone where they can tend
To all your pains, where all dogs end.

Up there, high above,
Gazing upon me, is the town,
Where bright colours shine down.

You will sit and wait
Until that fateful day,
When me and you are reunited
Side by side we will be
You're forever loyal to me.

There we will walk
Loving each other,
Until eternity comes to a stop,
As over Rainbow Bridge we cross.

Amy Wadsworth (12)
Ashlawn School, Rugby

The Wolf

The wolf howled to the midnight sky,
and to all the birds flying by.

The rest of his pack were hunting for food,
which left the wolf in a cheerful mood.

When they returned with a mouthful of rats,
the hour was late and they were covered in bats.

In the morning the wolves ran away,
because they don't like the light of a sunny day.

They hide themselves till the next night,
When they will prowl and start a fight.

Laura Barratt (13)
Ashlawn School, Rugby

A Seagull's Life

She silently falls, swiftly and slowly,
Through the night sky, quietly and lonely,
Gracefully sweeping the water's edge,
Then swooping up to the horizon's edge.

Flying here and flying there,
A lovely breeze from her gentle winged hair,
Flying far and flying near,
Water flowing calmly in the rear.

Sun's rising up to a lovely dawn,
A gentle breeze beginning to form,
The soft, crumbly, golden sand,
Searching for food she comes to land.

She silently falls, swiftly and slowly,
Through the night sky, quietly and lonely,
Gracefully sweeping the water's edge,
Then swooping up to the horizon's edge.

Laura Dunn (12)
Ashlawn School, Rugby

Painting A World

Dip my wand into the imagination.
My mind empties into the abyss, thoughts begin to appear.
The corruption that surrounds seems to fade away.
And the world rushes by, forgetting that I stand here.
Emotions and dreams are given a face.
I am the inventor of my creativity.
The power beneath the fingertips.

Abbey Grocott (12)
Ashlawn School, Rugby

A Tree's Day

I am so tall, I can touch the sky,
The wind is so strong like a devil in Hell.
I get hit and whipped, it hurts, oh my.
Then I can't wait for the final bell,
At last some piece and quiet,
But I am waiting for another riot.

Jack Cannell (12)
Ashlawn School, Rugby

Ice Hockey

As I skated around the rink,
I suddenly started to think,
Will I be good or will I be bad?
Will it hurt if the puck hits my pad?
As he went to take the shot,
I got told to mark the slot.
He then quickly fired the puck,
All I did was stand and look.
The puck got blasted off a skate,
As he came off, his foot was a state.

I sat and watched from the side,
I knew deep down I hadn't tried,
So I knew I had to try harder,
I knew I was as I grew sweatier,
I just got slammed against the glass,
I thought to myself, *you'll get a bash.*
I knew that the game was nearly done,
And that my team had just won.

Kyle Batchelor (13)
Ashlawn School, Rugby

Evil Butterfly

Beware of the evil butterfly,
It can take your life in the blink of an eye.
Like the Devil in disguise,
You can see the anger in her eyes.
No need to scream,
No need to shout,
The world stands still when she's about,
Carefully creeping around your home,
Looking for someone to call her own.
Beware of the evil butterfly,
Misunderstood and waiting to die.

Rebecca Goodyer (13)
Ashlawn School, Rugby

The World At War

The world is a dominant gene,
It lives as it dies,
The American Embassy works as it lies,
The power opens a whole lot of eyes.

This war rages, how long can it go?
The bullets from the monsters flow and flow,
The soldiers move forward as the silence arises,
The silence brings with it the last flying crow.

The innocent citizens run for their lives,
The lonely sun-dried land left for the flies,
The only last thing that has yet to survive,
The crooked hands grasp the dead,
They are thrown, the rest have fled.

Alex Bolland (13)
Ashlawn School, Rugby

King Of The Jungle

King of the jungle, towering above,
showing no compassion or any love.

A born leader that's what they all say,
reigning above them, no one dares get in his way.

They hunt for him, they pray for him,
but they long to break away,
knowing that they can't,
leaves them empty every day.

In the morning when the sunlight comes,
a pool of red, a sad tune hummed.

The body of the king lies limp and weak,
killed at the hands of the trust he couldn't keep.

Natasha Bourne (12)
Ashlawn School, Rugby

Just Dreaming

I looked at the blue yonder,
I saw the fishes swimming with me.
I knew I wasn't there.
I knew I was just having a dream, but I couldn't stop.
I had to go on fantasising.

I saw pink, green, yellow and blue.
All scampering and swaying along.
Then a gloomy, murky shadow falls above my head,
I don't bother to look up because I know what it is.

I swim and swim for my life as its tail slaps me as I turn.
No one is there to help me but then I see a gleam, a patch of light,
Like a star shining bright.
It holds back the monster just in time,
As it clenches its teeth at me with dirt and grime.

By the sound of its gills you can tell, the beast was calm.
He let it go and it swam and whimpered away.
The boy looked at me with his crystal-blue eyes
And golden hair sweeping over his forehead as I gazed at him,
But then I knew I was just dreaming.

Mayuri Patel (12)
Ashlawn School, Rugby

War

In glittering shells they came on white stallions,
The sun reflecting off their manes.
The knights drew their swords with a swing and cut down the enemy,
So fast, they didn't feel a thing.

Then came the foot soldiers, with axes up high,
And when they made contact, let them down with a heavy sigh.
Blood and guts went flying everywhere,
With the putrid smell of death filling the air.

And then the archers, losing their arrows,
Killing enough people to fill 50 barrows!
Then they were advancing, picking arrows from the ground,
By then the enemy knew their fate was bound.

Jay Francis-Wint (12)
Ashlawn School, Rugby

Noise

The scream of a falling tree
The whisper in the dark
The kiss of an angel
The sizzling of a spark

The rustle of leaves
The sting of a nettle
The footsteps on the grass
The whistle of a kettle

The ripping of paper
The tapping of feet
The smashing of glass
The music's constant beat

The clapping of an audience
The sound of a band
The cheer from a crowd
The helicopter's deafening land

The slaughter of a victim
The scream of pain
The cut on the wrist
That shows no gain

The bang of a firework
The slam of a door
The chatter in the jungle
The lion's mighty roar

The tiptoe of a worm
The swoop of wings
The holding of hands
The quietest of things

The crescendo of noise surrounds us,
And what you hear now is silence . . .

Again.

Kat Cooney (12)
Ashlawn School, Rugby

My Mad Grandma

I have a grandma
Who is slightly mad
She likes to sing
About a mad king
She also likes to dance about
Doing hip hop like I don't know what.

With her friends she goes out
Playing and mucking about.
Her friends are the same,
A little bit strange,
Acting like teenagers do.

But I don't care
If my grandma is weird,
Because she is the best grandma
In the world!

Fiona Betts (13)
Ashlawn School, Rugby

Gymnastics

Full spin and flick,
Forward tummy, if I'm quick,
Handspring into splits,
Point my toes as I go in the pit.
Now I have to touch the line,
Before I run out of time.

Remembering my beat,
I best make it neat,
Three judges staring at me,
Looking at me as far as they can see.
Finish it off with that super turn,
I've been practising for this, I need to learn.
Will I make it,
Or will I just get hit?
I stumble to my feet,
And I walk to my seat.
The judges give me points,
Will my place be joint?
They're about to say the places,
And then I see their faces,
They get everyone's attention and say,
'The winner is . . .'

Katie Braithwaite (14)
Ashlawn School, Rugby

In English

I look outside the window,
The rain is lashing it down,
Lightning illuminates the dark grey sky.
And the thunder makes a loud explosion.

I am sitting inside my English room,
Writing this poem,
Staring out of the window,
Looking for inspiration.

The pitter-patter of the rain,
The regular claps of thunder,
Are giving me a splitting headache,
And we still have 35 minutes until break.

Luke Horrocks (14)
Ashlawn School, Rugby

Desert

The sun rose in the sky as high as can be.
The rays beat down hard upon me!
The sand is scattered on the floor, as dry as a bone.
Stepping, stepping, keep on going, I'm so far from home.
I am tired and longing for a drink,
Ten miles ahead a town, I think!
The desert stretches out far ahead,
I am dying, dying, dying, dead!

Izzy McLaren (13)
Ashlawn School, Rugby

Louis Philippe

L ively as the wind in a storm
O utside like a tree in the wilderness
U tter disappointment to cancellations and un-involvement
I nspired by many different things
S arcastic and humorous

P erfect can't be used to describe me
H istory, I hope to make it in this world
I s there a sport I don't know how to play?
L ost in my imagination half of the time
I' m always up for new challenges
P ast and future, all reflection
P ast regrets I don't let bother me or haunt me
E very day is as exciting as the next.

Louis-Philippe Delaugere (12)
Ashlawn School, Rugby

Another Rainy Day

Today it is raining cats and dogs
the rain is so heavy and powerful
it will soak us through
be we don't have a clue.

It is a dull, dark day
with nothing to play
all we can do is sit inside
and find a place to hide.

The thunder is crashing
the rain is lashing
the lightning is flashing
and everyone is moaning.

There is no colour around
everything is black and white
all we hear is a loud sound
and people screaming with fright.

Why did it have to come
on the day of Interform?
Why couldn't the sun come out
and dry the rain out?

Viresh Mistry (14)
Ashlawn School, Rugby

Rain

The rain fell hard against the ground,
It was getting heavier and heavier,
I could hear the sound on the roof,
It was loud.

It ran down the windows,
And hit the window ledges,
The sound of thunder,
And a sudden flash.

Everywhere outside was wet,
So I couldn't go out,
I had to say inside,
Just staring out at the rain.

The thunder got louder,
The lightning got brighter,
The rain got heavier,
When all of a sudden,

It all stopped,
There was no noise,
There was no flashing,
There was no rain.

The sun came out,
And lightened up the sky,
Everything dried up,
And I went out.

Chloe Williams (13)
Ashlawn School, Rugby

Prey

He marched,
he crouched like a shadow of the night,
each blade of grass was a shelter from sight,
the grass was tall,
the moon was high,
ready to strike,
the moment was nigh.
Closer and closer,
he crept up behind,
he gracefully pounced
only to find . . .
the target was quick,
too quick to catch,
so he turned in disgust,
he turned and went back.

He was cold,
but he didn't care,
he glanced forward and noticed a bear!
Was this the end?
Was death so near?
He stood on a rock,
pain over-ran fear,
he turned to the left,
no more mood,
he would have had energy if he had had food.
He slowed to a stop,
he had to fight,
the tiger fought bravely throughout the night.
It finished and although he had won,
he was wounded . . .
his life was gone.

Gene Parker-Brombley (13)
Ashlawn School, Rugby

The Fat Cat

Every day eating away, asking for more,
It was like a giant bouncy ball,
Big, round, with a strange square head,
Acting like he had never been fed.

If it wanted to travel, it would roll not walk,
You could see people staring, starting to talk,
If a car got in its way there would be hell to pay,
But the cat would keep on rolling.

The people of London thought it was an earthquake,
People running relentlessly, like they had seen a snake,
People from Manchester could feel it,
The thunder would start when the cat would sit.

Elliott Youds (13)
Ashlawn School, Rugby

My Nightmare World

Is . . . dark, damp and abandoned,
Black, blurred shadows in the distance,
It's a terrifying thunderstorm at night.
Nobody to love and nobody's comfort,
A day in the life of a criminal or devil.
It's the blinding stench of a sewer,
A world crawling with unpleasant grime,
It's a place I never want to visit again.

Ella Slatcher (13)
Ashlawn School, Rugby

Alien Teachers

The teachers at school are aliens, I swear!
One of them is even a mutant bear.
I know you probably don't care,
But I tell you they have an evil lair.
Some have three or four eyes.
I told my mum but she said, 'Don't tell lies.'
So I told all the other guys,
But they kept eating those poisonous pies.
I hear them talk about their planet, Mars,
And all of their favourite stars.
I think they said they had flying cars,
The make was called Lars.
One day I had a detention with Mrs Glotton,
She had a tail out of her bottom.
Her husband looked like Batman from Gotham,
And her son looked like Robin from Gotham.
So all over our world there are creatures from space,
Like Linford Christie winning a race.
But just to tell you, you know, just in case,
I'm an alien who *loves* to eat and is from a strawberry lace.

Joe Fenwick-Wilson
Ashlawn School, Rugby

Every Day . . . Why?

Every day I feel sad,
In the dumps and really bad.
Where's my money? Where's my bike?
Where are the people that I like?
Look at the blood, the bruise, the scabs,
Look at the help that I really have to have.
Where's my dad? Where's my mum?
Help me now cos I'm not in the sun.
How long do I have to sit in the corner
Watching the days get longer and longer?
Help!

Alice Stewardson (11)
Ashlawn School, Rugby

Tears

I cry these tears for you,
but you shall never know.
I hide my fear from you,
my happiness will never show.

I gave my heart to you,
you lost it in the wind.
You went to look for it,
to put it in the bin.

I loved you once,
I love you still.
I always have,
and always will.

You've broke my heart,
it's bleeding so.
And your love for me,
Shall never show.

George Walshe
Ashlawn School, Rugby

The Spider

The spider of the night has an evil trick
to bite or does he? Or does he, maybe
he is lovely.

Seeing those thick black legs reminds me of rotten pegs.
Or maybe they are silky smooth with just a hint of groove.

Should I let my anger out with a jump,
scream and shout? Should I really say
goodbye to the ugly black thing that hides?

Under all that thick black hair, there's a handsome man in there.
Don't believe me, see for yourself and get a spider for wealth.

Or is this really true?
I don't know,
I've been asking you!

Frances Elliott (12)
Ashlawn School, Rugby

Victimised

Every time I close my eyes,
I fear waking up for school,
When I walk through the school gates
My nightmare begins!
I get tormented and teased,
I get poked fun at and called names.
Do they know how it feels?
I get stared at,
I'm the centre of attention,
- But for all the wrong reasons.
Every day I think to myself,
Who am I?
I'm nothing!
I'm worthless!
I'm a victim!

Laura Maybury (11)
Ashlawn School, Rugby

It's A Lie

He hit me,
He kicked me,
He stole my things,
I told a teacher,
He denied it,
It's a lie.

It got worse,
He punched me,
He took my money,
I told the head teacher,
He denied it,
It's a lie.

It got really upsetting,
He called me names,
He broke my things,
He got me into trouble,
I told my parents,
He dined it,
It's a lie.

I don't go to school any more,
I bunk off school because,
It's a lie,
It's a lie.

Kati Simpson (11)
Ashlawn School, Rugby

Bullying Me!

I walk up to school wishing that people won't say
What I dread the most every day.
Every time I shut my eyes, I see my pain itself.
The sadness which I feel,
Offending what they do,
For picking on me,
For bullying me, which upsets the way I feel.
For ganging up on people, for ganging up on me,
I've just got one question,
Why me?

Shaun Stuart (11)
Ashlawn School, Rugby

Bullies!

B ullies are sly, they make you cry.
U nder pressure because they are hurting me.
L onely, sad, cold and hungry.
L ooking at their fierce faces.
I nside a damp and dark place.
E very day at school this happens to me.
S ad, cold, lonely and still hungry.

Olivia Kelly (11)
Ashlawn School, Rugby

What Have I Done To You?

Why, why, why do you keep bullying me?
Why, why, why do you keep hurting me?
Why, why, why do you make me sad?
I can't take what you're doing to me.
I can't stand it anymore.
I can't wait for school to finish.
I just want this pain to finish.
Every day I get bullied, every day I'm sad.
Every day I get hurt I feel really mad.
Every day I cry.
Every day I wish to die.
I just want this day to end.

Thomas Swinford (11)
Ashlawn School, Rugby

Will It Ever End?

My life was at doom
as I stepped out the room,
so I cried, so I cried.
I was unfairly pushed,
my heart turned to mush,
so I cried, so I cried.
I hit back and yelled,
I was justly expelled,
so I cried, so I cried.
I couldn't tell my mum
and I had no chum,
so I cried.

Helena Crisford (12)
Ashlawn School, Rugby

Why? Why Me?

Why? Why me?
Today I got picked on
Like always.
Why do people say stuff?
Why do people say stuff about how I look?
It's always me.
They say
Ugly! Geek! Nerd! Coward!

Amanvir Nagra (11)
Ashlawn School, Rugby

Riverbank Love

Walking down the path, hand in hand, near the riverbank.
The grass dancing in the wind,
The sun following them.
All the clovers on the ground bring them good luck.
Let's hope they stay together!

Walking, walking, each step and breath brings new life.
Now they're running further down the bank, *splash!*
Throwing stones on the starry water,
All the ripples glistening in the sun,
Off they go under the blossomed trees,
The couple that care.

Lydia Iliff (13)
Ashlawn School, Rugby

What Is Love?

What is love?
It's something that's all around you,
It's something that makes you laugh,
It's something that makes you cry,
It's something you see in people's eyes,
It's something shared from friend to friend,
It's something shared from lover to lover,
It's something shared from another to another,
It's something that can only be one way sometimes
Because different people love you in different ways,
As a friend, as more than a friend,
As a family member, as a best mate,
But love is complicated,
Love is confusing,
Love can leave your heart in for a bruising,
But one thing I know is this,
Where would we be without it?
Where would I be without my family
To cherish and protect me?
Where would I be without my best friend?
Who's always there to help my heart mend.
Where would I be without the one I love?
Where would I ever be without the one I dream of . . .

Katie Irwin (13)
Ashlawn School, Rugby

Untitled

My nightmare world is . . .
dark, damp and abandoned,
black blurry shadows in the distance,
it's a terrifying thunderstorm at night,
nobody to love and nobody's comfort,
a day in the life of a criminal or a devil,
it's the blinding stench of a sewer,
a world crawling with unpleasant grime,
it's a place I never want to visit!

Maddie Riddell (13)
Ashlawn School, Rugby

Rolling

Rolling, rolling,
I'm always rolling,
It's all I ever do.
The empty space is filled now,
Up and down I go,
Will I ever stop rolling?
The answer is no,
Rolling, rolling,
It's my favourite thing to do.
My passion, my hobby,
My life, my way,
Rolling, rolling,
I'm always rolling.

Jordan Evans **(13)**
Ashlawn School, Rugby

It

It stared at me,
It stared with its enormous eyes.
It stared at me,
It stared through the window.

It looked upset,
It had tears rolling down its face,
It looked upset,
It was begging me.

It needed me,
It wanted me to open the door,
It needed me,
It felt unloved,
It needed me,
It wanted me to help it.

It lay down,
Giving up,
It lay down,
Feeling that nobody cared,
It lay down,
Wondering what it had done wrong.

It was Tiska,
My dog, my best friend,
It was Tiska,
Locked outside, I had to help it.

Shaun Boulter (13)
Ashlawn School, Rugby

My Teenage Life

I wake up in the morning, snoring and yawning.
My hamster wants food, by God it looked good.
It gave a big smile just for a while.
I got dressed but I was really stressed.
I forgot my homework, a detention I'll get,
As I stared at my pet.
I had my meal, some money I steal,
I think my bro spotted me though
But he never really cares.
I rushed to school,
Sometimes it's cool.
English is a piece of cake
With the jokes Sir makes.
My friends are just cool,
They can be just fools.
I got home tired, when my heart gets retired.
I go on MSN, I talk to my friends.
They cheer me up, then they make me hyper,
With a baby's diaper.
I go to bed, with my sleepy head,
Dream of this girl, who rocks my world!

Shehzaad Mullah (13)
Ashlawn School, Rugby

ASBO Poem

ASBOs
Chavs and emos
Townies and trendies
Goths and crazies
Who's who?
Nobody knows
But who really cares?
Teenagers don't . . . it's just something to talk about.
People always blame the first person they see . . .
It's usually a teenager
If the local shop gets robbed . . .
If someone's house gets egged . . .
You guessed, it's usually a teenager
Nobody listens, nobody cares
But we are the future!

Josh Hammond (13)
Ashlawn School, Rugby

She Left Us

She left us her paw prints to follow
She left her warmth to keep us company
She left all her memories behind so we can find them.

She left her voice for us to chase
She left her picture for us to gaze
She left us her toy so we could hold.

She left the sound of her footsteps so we could wait
She left her blanket so we could touch
She left her dark days so we could brighten them up.

She left the blossoms blossoming
She left us wishing she was still here.

Zainab Mogul (14)
Ashlawn School, Rugby

A Purrfect Friend!

As he sat on my lap
So happy and sweet
With his heart beating with joy
Without a care in the world

Overflowing with love
As I hugged him gently
His soft fur up against me
So huggably soft

He leaped out my arms
And ran into the night
With a moonlit sky

I paused
Tears down my face
As there he lay
My best friend
My cat
Bradley.

Helen Gibson (13)
Ashlawn School, Rugby

Someone Special

Her hair as brown as dark chocolate
Her eyes as deep as water
Her skin as smooth as softly sewn silk
Her heart is made of gold
Her caring hands look after me
Comfort me when I'm down
She makes me feel special
When my heart is feeling sad
We have become so close over these years
It's something before I've never had
And now because we have
It shall never disappear
She's the best mum you can ever have
For the rest of those years.

Melanie Johnson (15)
Ashlawn School, Rugby

My Poem

I walked in and he was there
That filth giving me that evil stare
I wanted to knock him out
But couldn't because I'd get a clout
Lazy man sitting on my sofa
I wanted him out so it was over.

My sis came in
There my face lit up with a grin
There he goes running his mouth
Calling her a yardie, that got her mad so she gave him a clout
Now there he goes thinking he's cool
But he got slapped up, he's just a fool
I thought to myself he's lucky it weren't my brother
Because he would have been laid out like no other
Lazy bloke got out of bed
Went to town hammered out of his head
Cheeked some guy in the Monastery Rooms
He hits the floor as the flower blooms.

Grant Spooner-Roberts (15)
Ashlawn School, Rugby

Climbing The Ladder

One child
Six bullies
One child
No friends

Break times
Six bullies
Break time
No friends

Lunch time
Another victim
Lunch time
One friend

Class time
One teacher
Class time
Two friends

Home time
Your parents
Home time
Four friends

Katie King (11)
Ashlawn School, Rugby

Bullying Is Very Bad

Bullying is something that is harmful,
It is never forgettable,
If it's happening to you,
Then you know what to do,
You should go and tell a teacher.

Bullying is very bad,
Because it makes everyone feel sad.
If they call you nasty names,
Then they are very lame.

Kiran Dhariwal (11)
Ashlawn School, Rugby

It Never Ends

The last time I had some fun
Was 3 years ago.

I am scared to go to school
Because of my old friends.

The last time I had some food at school
Was 5 years ago.

The last time I walked to school
Was 5 years ago.

Every day I come home crying.

I want everyone to stop,
But they won't.
Stop now, please!

Ben Hollis (12)
Ashlawn School, Rugby

Help Me!

Bullying is something that makes you hurt,
Something that makes you feel alone,
Bullying is something that completely destroys you,
But if you tell a teacher,
All your problems will *disappear!*

Sonny Griffiths-Lynch (11)
Ashlawn School, Rugby

Untitled

I don't want to go to school today
To be bullied this way.
It's the time of day when I want to be dead.
I am being bullied as we speak,
Kicked, punched, names and more.

I am a child, not a punch bag,
I am scared,
I look round every corner
In case they're there.

Ryan Sabin (11)
Ashlawn School, Rugby

Stop The Bullying

I don't want to go to school today,
'Cause I know I'll just get bullied,
could I have a friend,
someone to be there for me?

Why am I bullied anyway?
I should be able to stand up and say,
leave me alone
but I'm too scared to pick up the phone.

Stop the bullying
let people feel at home.

Scott Crisp (11)
Ashlawn School, Rugby

Bully

B is for bullying me
U is for being unkind to me
L is for lying to me
L is for laughing at me when I'm hurt
Y is for, 'Oi you, come here!'

Liam Reynolds (11)
Ashlawn School, Rugby

I Am Lost

I am lost,
And never found.
I am dead
No, only numb.
Lost in the abyss that is my school.
Stop.
Please stop,
And then I will rock.
I may look different,
Act different,
Speak different,
But there's no difference.
Only you may bring me back,
And the bullies will crack.
Just as I fall to my knees.
Stop.
Full stop!

Daniel Francis (11)
Ashlawn School, Rugby

Bullying

I don't want to go to school today,
Because I don't have any friends
I'm lonely, I'm friendless.
All alone with nobody to play with me,
Nobody likes me.
It's horrible to keep being alive,
I wish I were dead.
My life is hysterical, evil and cruel.

If you are alone,
There's no need to moan,
'Cause there's people around the world just like you.

Beth Lawrence (11)
Ashlawn School, Rugby

Being A Bully

Being a bully is a bad thing.
You might not know you're being a bully,
So try not to be one.

Racism, physical abuse, verbal abuse is bullying.

Terry Morgans (11)
Ashlawn School, Rugby

Day After Day . . .

I don't want to go to school today,
Or the day after that or the day after that.

Endless days with the terror that took
My life away from me.

That bribed my parents,
That looked so innocent,
That killed me,
That banished me from the classroom,
That stopped my life.

I don't want to go to school today,
In fact I don't want to live.

Nikesh Patel (11)
Ashlawn School, Rugby

My Days In Jamaica

In Jamaica we never
sit on the grass, but we smoke
it!
When the sun is hot and the
trees are green
The coconut tree weeps
by the sea.
We eat up all our
rice and peas,
and we even have our
own bobsleigh team.

The dry hot climate and the
hot white sand is the place
to be when the reggae band
come by.
They bang on the bongos and the steel pans combine,
As we drink up
all our rum and wine.

Alex Kerr (15)
Ashlawn School, Rugby

Untitled

I was departing for sunny Ibiza,
I was buzzing with excitement, as if I were in ecstasy.
The sun was rising and not a cloud to be seen,
Oh if only I had a bud on which to lean.
And the grass was green,
Of my mother I did dream,
I walked on the beach,
Where I walked the sand was burning my feet whilst I did talk.
I could hear the sound of a tongue
Which was blowing my mind.
I needed to be gone,
Before I took that shotgun
And pulled the trigger,
Which would not be fun.

David Morgan (15)
Ashlawn School, Rugby

Tokyo

Tokyo is the place to be
If you want some sushi
The bustling sounds of the big city
As it's seen on Japanese TV

If you want something high-tech
Tokyo is the place to check
If you want to see something bling
Head on down to the sumo ring

The bullet train goes lightning fast
You won't even notice it go past
The buildings all standing tall
With neon lights upon the wall.

Aaron Stonard (15)
Ashlawn School, Rugby

Untitled

The hot glistening sun beaming on Earth
I am neither south nor north
I am having a dream holiday
Home is close not far away
No early morning
I'm out when the sun is dawning
Out on the beach drinking rum
The locals having fun with me and everyone
Sinking my feet into the sand
Wishing I didn't have to go back to England.

Tom Curley (15)
Ashlawn School, Rugby

Best Friends

Smiles, tears, giggles and laughs
Late night calls and cute photographs
I'll be there for you till the day
Of my death, best friends forever
Till my very last breath

We have been there for each other
Through thick and thin
We can tell each other everything
You're the best friend a girl could have
All I am trying to say is
I hope we stay
Best friends for all my days.

Amy Morris (13)
Ashlawn School, Rugby

My Mum

She's a young, hip, fresh mum
that always like to sing.
She has a mobile phone that always rings, ring, ring, ring.
She goes out and has a laugh
always likes to brag.
Until one day she came back and said
she had lost her bag.

She is a young, hip, fresh mum
that always likes to dance,
she will dance to rap, garage, pop and trance.
My mum is a good mum
and I am happy with that!

Samantha Clarke (13)
Ashlawn School, Rugby

Seasons

Animals come out of hibernation
Birds come back to brighten the nation
Trees shoot leaves, flowers grow
Lambing season starts to flow

Days are hotter, nights are shorter
Now is the time to fight with water
Summer holidays soon to come
Soon we'll play in sand and sun

Nights grow longer, it's getting cold now
Animals prepare, they have the know-how
They find their food and warmth before
The winter comes to chill their core

Christmas comes but once a year
The trees are bare, the snow is here
Wrap up warm, it's cold out there
A warm chocolate drink for us to share.

Leslie Clarke (12)
Ashlawn School, Rugby

Africa

The loud roar of the tribal music
Made by bongo drums
That blocks the red-hot intensity of the desert sun
As it shines like a magnifying glass
Burning a harmless ant.

The lazy meercat bathes by the waterfall
All nice and cool.
They are as lazy as a gorilla
Lying after a day eating.
Once the meercats stop they prepare for the breeding season
For in the wild as a new life begins
The race for survival begins.

Ryan Welburn (12)
Ashlawn School, Rugby

Africa

The sun is as hot as an oven
The drums beat like a gorilla
The dry deserts dazzle in drought
The waterfalls soar

The stampedes sound like an aeroplane
The baby birds rest on the elephants
The slithery snake slides up the slimy stone.

Reuben Desouza (11)
Ashlawn School, Rugby

The Other World

A nimals in the world
F riendships between cultures
R eligious tribes from different areas
I mages of poverty and hurt
C ocoa beans flood the forests
A frica is a different world.

Robert Barnett (11)
Ashlawn School, Rugby

Africa

Rocks rolling off mountains
Like hippos in the black mud.
Three seconds go by
As a few souls die.
Rhinos are lightning bolts,
Hurdling over broken bones of their prey.

Life to death as the dusty mud
Gets in their annoyed faces
Bang, bang!
Drums crash.
Monkeys swing from tree to tree,
And they are crazy as hyenas.
When nightfall comes
And the skies go blue,
Mother Nature can never go to sleep,
As the night creatures come out and stand tall.

Nicole Gulliver (11)
Ashlawn School, Rugby

African

A load of wondrous music
F riday's for your music as Sundays are for your Sunday roast
R ice is our favourite meal like chicken is yours
 I n our language we write *hi* in a number of letters
C reated new life
A lot of nice weather, not much rain
N ature is common, animals are like the sun, priceless.

Vishan Parmar (11)
Ashlawn School, Rugby

Africa

Hear the sounds of the African music,
The beat of the drums to the animal sounds,
Hear the sounds of the waterfall flowing,
The splish and splash of the animals trudging.

See the stampedes, charging around,
See the buffaloes and the rhinos leading the crowd.
See the landscape from every direction,
The mountains, waterfalls in every single section.

Denise Bladon (11)
Ashlawn School, Rugby

Africa

Animals run wild,
over the desert plains,
but over here,
the animals are on reins.

Weather is so hot,
it is like a boiling pot,
plains are so pretty,
with lovely waterfalls.

Animals are lovely
they shouldn't be poached.
Animals are born,
their fur is not to be worn.

Nature is a place of quiet,
it shouldn't be disturbed.
Nature is a beautiful thing,
so please don't hurt it.

Music is cool,
but in Africa it is full of thoughts.
In Africa it is a daily thing,
it is their beliefs.

Alexandra Lawton (11)
Ashlawn School, Rugby

Bullying

I am a cobweb sitting in the corner of the toilets,
There's something going on,
There's a child shedding tears,
As a larger person is calling him names.
I don't know what is happening, but the big one's holding a fag,
He's also got a phone.
If I look a bit closer I can just make out,
'Come down to the loos as I'm bullying a kid.'
I wonder what he's doing to that poor child,
Wait! He's threatening him for dinner money,
I hope the child gives it to him,
And goes to tell a teacher.
Ahh, the big kids are leaving,
Just thank God for that.
Now go and tell the teacher!

Matthew Threadgold (11)
Ashlawn School, Rugby

New Life

The sun is a ball of fire
Beaming down on new life
The African drums are playing
The tribal members are signing for new life
Animals bow down to the prince
Elephants stamping
Monkeys jumping
And exotic birds chirping for new life
Graceful giraffes
And resting lionesses
Praise new life.

Scarlett John (11)
Ashlawn School, Rugby

Africa Ya Ajabu

The lion is born,
At the rise of the scorching sun,
While gazing at the plains,
Animals crowded like birds with meat,
Drums are elephants stamping their feet,
While insects eat,
The sun will set,
The animals will sleep until morn.

Evangeline Wheeler-Jones (11)
Ashlawn School, Rugby

Help

I was sitting on my own,
Thinking alone,
My brain was buzzing,
My heart was pounding.

I was approached by a gang,
All were tall and slim,
I was scared,
I didn't know what to do.

I looked up to see,
My ex best friend,
Part of the gang,
I had to think for a moment to realise what was going on.

There was no escape,
I was shouting for help,
But no one responded,
I then realised when I looked up there was my friend.

She had seen it all,
I was trying to tell her what was going on,
She got the message and went to
Tell the teacher, of course straight away.

The next day I heard that they had been excluded,
So think next time,
If you are being bullied,
Go and tell the teacher straight away!

Eleanor Garside (11)
Ashlawn School, Rugby

Bullying Is . . .

B ullying is mean and cruel.
U nfortunately bullying is happening every day.
L ittle do we know that more people suffer from bullying each week.
L ots of teachers have to try to make their schools bully free.
Y oung people and old get bullied each day.
I n fact everyone is vulnerable to getting hurt mentally by bullies.
N ormally bullies just want to cover up their own feelings.
G enerally bullies are just mean cowards!

Indeed, we all feel vulnerable to others, but . . .
Some people just put up with bullying and don't tell.

Tell someone you know straight away!

Chloe Bell (11)
Ashlawn School, Rugby

He Hits, He Laughs, I Scream

I'm standing in the hallway,
Knowing I'll get hurt.
He's coming round the corner,
Shouting, 'Little squirt.'

I'm hoping it's not real,
Maybe it's a dream?
He's standing right in front of me,
He hits, he laughs, I scream!

Harley Childs (11)
Ashlawn School, Rugby

Stop, Please Stop

I am a bird, I can feel everything.
I feel you getting hurt,
I feel the blood dripping down your face,
Your arms, your legs, everywhere.
It hurts just to think about it.
Stop, please stop.

I can hear everything.
I can hear you scream for help,
I can hear you shout
And the punch that just hit you.
Stop, please stop.

I can taste everything.
I can taste the blood dripping,
From your nose into your mouth.
And when you fall to the ground
I can taste the grass
Where someone has just pushed you.
Stop, please stop!

Please stop!

Mollie Brind (11)
Ashlawn School, Rugby

My Terrible Secret

It is horrible, my terrible secret.
I've kept it for so, so long,
I've never told a soul,
I never will, I can't,
My terrible secret.

It isn't gossip, my terrible secret,
And it's nothing at all glamorous.
It's gruesome, dark and cruel.
My terrible secret.

It must be so hard for her,
I see it every day,
They hit her, punch her,
That is my terrible secret.

They take all her lunch money,
They shout and call her names,
But I'm too cowardly to tell anyone,
So it shall always be my terrible secret.

Bethany-Jade Stratford (11)
Ashlawn School, Rugby

Racism

R uining people's lives
A cting hard in front of your mates, taking the mickey
C alling people names because of their skin
I nsulting people for their colour
S aying harmful things that could upset them
M ake sure you respect and select anybody for a friend

But never reflect on someone's skin.

Aaron Mills (12)
Ashlawn School, Rugby

Bullying

I am a fly, this is what I think bullying is . . .
Bullying is cruel,
Bullying is mean,
This is definitely the worst I have ever seen!
I am sat on a victim's back,
The villain has chucked him in a sack.
He started to shake with fear,
But he could run as fast as a deer.
He ran as fast as he could,
And as well he should!

Hannah Swinford (11)
Ashlawn School, Rugby

Bullying

There is a bully outside, bullying someone,
From the victim's point of view it isn't much fun.
People say bullying is nasty and cruel,
And everyone thinks he should be kicked out of school.
We try to be friendly and just say, 'Hi,'
But the bully's got a problem, we don't know why.
Lock him in the cellar,
Throw away the key,
No games, no consoles, no TV.
Finally someone told the teacher and the bully was gone,
And now without him the school proudly shone.

Kishan Vaghela (11)
Ashlawn School, Rugby

The Bee On The Roof

I can see a bully, he looks like a wimp,
The victim acting like a bin,
Lips of the bully, sharp and tight,
The boy waiting for the bully to start a fight.
I feel sad as well for the prisoner,
I know he feels sad, sad, sad.
The bully should be feeling so bad.
The bully will be touched by the sting,
Once I've got him I'm sure he'll go ping.
The smell of chocolate, alcohol and Coke,
I really think the bully just had a smoke.
The taste is dirty, the boy is scared,
Now the bully is dared.
The fight is won,
The game is done,
It was the victim with the glory,
And that's the end of the story.

Lewis Cutts (11)
Ashlawn School, Rugby

The Bee On The Wall

I can see hatred in the bully's eyes as he shoves her to the ground,
I can sense evil all around, in the air,
I can touch her pain as if it was mine.

But what can I do, I'm just the bee on the wall?

I can feel her heart beating,
Faster as she gets dragged along the floor,
I can smell the Devil around me,
I can taste the fear streaming past my lips.

But what can I do, I'm just the bee on the wall?

Ellie Collins (11)
Ashlawn School, Rugby

Bullying

B ullying is a common effect on today's society
U nlike most people some people put up with bullying
L ying is a common way to hurt the victim's feelings
L uckily a lot of children are brave enough to tell someone
Y ou, the children of the world, 60% of you are not bullied,

the other 40% are

I think bullying should be stopped
N o one or nothing should tolerate bullying
G irls get bullied just because of their appearance.

Jessica Edkins (11)
Ashlawn School, Rugby

Casper

Just a few years through sun and rain,
how soon his days were done.
We're left with but a memory
of his love for everyone.

He wasn't just a handsome dog,
with a love that would not bend,
not just a family member,
but an ever loyal friend.

We can no longer see him,
or hear his welcome bark,
but he will still be with us,
when all around seems dark.

For through his love he left for us,
a gift that will not end,
the ever present memory
of an ever loyal friend.

Sam Tuckey (15)
Ashlawn School, Rugby

I Can

I can smell the coldness of the bully's cold heart.
I can hear the whimpering of the punched young boy.
I can see the young boy, who was punched, crying.
I cannot see the point of bullying.
I can see the point of telling the teacher if you're bullied.
I cannot see the point of racism.
I cannot see the point of punching people or fighting.

George Clark (11)
Ashlawn School, Rugby

Bullying

B ullying is not very nice.

U s people who are being bullied are not impressed

L ying to get yourself out of trouble.

L eaving marks is not very nice.

Y ou are very cruel.

I f you think you can escape being in trouble, you're wrong.

N ot very pleased are teachers.

G oing home and feeling guilty.

Lloyd Briggs (11)
Ashlawn School, Rugby

Bullying

I'm a fly, flying by.
I sat upon a wall,
Then I heard someone start to cry,
I saw a boy about to fall.

The boy on the floor was really sad,
Then another boy stole his hat,
The boy on the floor looked really bad,
The boy stood up from where he sat.

The big boy ran away,
The small boy had nothing to say.
The small boy was very still,
And he looked very ill.

Sam Colledge (11)
Ashlawn School, Rugby

Bullying In School

I fear the word school,
For others, school is cool,
But for me it's just another day,
Where I get beaten.

I come to school knowing,
I have no friends,
But for me it's just another day,
On my own.

I love the feeling of leaving,
For it warms me up,
But I still have another three weeks ahead,
And they will be tough.

I come to school knowing,
I will be lonely,
I will be beaten,
But tomorrow I will not be returning.

Akshay Vaghela (11)
Ashlawn School, Rugby

Bully

B e on the lookout for bullying,
U pper school might attack,
L ower school be on alert for bullying,
L ook left and right if upper school are coming,
Y es, I have been surrounded and I am going to be attacked.

Dilan Mistry (11)
Ashlawn School, Rugby

The Bully

I saw him, standing there, he suddenly came up to me,
I tried to run but he punched me, I went down on my knees.
He kicked me,
It hurt.

He picked me up,
Took my lunch money,
Then dropped me.

After that I don't know what happened,
Then I awoke in hospital.

I was told he was suspended for 2 months.
That made me feel better.
When he came back to me, he ran.
And that was the end of that bully.

Emily Dixon (11)
Ashlawn School, Rugby

Bullying

B ullying is the worst thing in the world
U nfortunately people get hurt
L aughing, laughing, the bullies laugh
L eaving the victim behind
Y elling help, the victim cries
I n the end the bullies run
N ot getting caught by anyone
G etting up the victim cries.

Anisa Patel (11)
Ashlawn School, Rugby

Bullying

B lackmailing is not very nice to other people
U sing people, if you do that you're not very nice
L ying to people is not nice, because it means a sly person
L eaving people out is not nice, because it's best if you are friends
Y ou must treat everyone as you would want to be treated
I nternet is a bad thing, because you can say racist comments
N ame-calling is a bad thing, because you hurt people's feelings
G rabbing other people's belongings for money is bad.

Joe Beasley (12)
Ashlawn School, Rugby

Power Change

Every day instructions
constantly given
directions, work needed
no choice
total control of me
go home
lots of homework to do
sister comes
I get to see her baby
hold her
I'm now in control
finally, but
is baby wholly in control?
Probably not.

Felicity Webb (16)
Ashlawn School, Rugby

Untitled

Her long brown hair
Makes all the boys stare

Her gorgeous face
Sends me to space

Her big hazel eyes
As clear as the skies

She makes me smile
Sometimes frown, without
Her I would always be down

Without her I would be blue
I love every little thing we do
I want to be with her always
Stuck together like glue

I'll give away a little clue
Her name is Rachel.

Chris Givelin (15)
Ashlawn School, Rugby

That Day

That day's the day that changed my life.
It's the day when nothing makes sense.
It's the day when the meaning of pain was doubled.
It's the day when everything changed.

That day's the day that changed my life.
Like the sun when it ceases to be in the sky for one long night.
And then it rises, yet the clouds are blocking out its warm rays.
It's a day when I'm stuck in one place.

It's a day that turns into weeks.
But it's that one day that changes everything.
The routine I'm in
The way I live.
The things I do, just for those weeks, my life turned upside down.

And then I'm stuck
In this beautiful country.
But all I want to do is get out. Let me go, let me go.

That day was the day that changed my life.

Jessica Holton (15)
Ashlawn School, Rugby

Babysitting For You

In a house, miles from home,
watching you playing, pretty in pink.

You climb the sofa landing on your toys
you're only a year but so full of noise.

As you weep and moan wanting a bottle,
I go to kitchen to make you some juice.

As you spill it down your pretty pink dress
your mother comes home and sends you to bed.

Melissa Manani (15)
Ashlawn School, Rugby

My Dad

When I'm crying about you,
I'm crying to you,
Even if you can't hear me,
I always wish you were still here.
I wish you could come back,
And open your arms,
And tell me it's going to be OK.
But I know you can't.

These last few years have been difficult,
All the tears I cried, all the pain I felt,
Won't go away.
I thought you would never leave,
I thought you would be here to watch me grow up
The way you would want me to.

Danielle Wills (15)
Ashlawn School, Rugby

Gavin

I think about your glossy brown hair,
Your blue eyes that sparkle just like the night sky you're so fond of,
And your warming smile that always gave me a sign of hope,
I always thought you'd be able to cope.

We miss you so much,
And often wonder why you haven't kept in touch.
Your memory is so clear,
If only you were just as near.

Maybe you're better off away from this place,
It's become such a disgrace,
Yeah . . . it's a nicer place where you are,
Close to the shining stars,
You're our shining star,
Shine on.

Chéy Kirby (15)
Ashlawn School, Rugby

Tell Me

Ever wanted to tell someone something,
but you knew it would be the hardest thing ever?

You love them so much,
and you know it's the right thing to do,
but you want to protect them from the truth.

Pretending doesn't work,
denying doesn't work,
forgetting doesn't work.
It always comes back and takes control of your mind.

In the corridor, laughing and joking with friends,
as soon as you're alone, past ghosts appear.
You try to fight them away,
fists flying,
tears pouring,
foul words,
nothing works.
You're still left alone with your wounds, crying.
Friends can only do so much.
They're just as scared as you are.
I did tell someone, but now they want me to tell you.
I want to, but how can I disappoint you like that?

I know what happened wasn't my fault,
by not telling I'm protecting you from the truth.
But I know you should know.
I can never forget what happened,
I will tell you one day.

It's just that I love you Mum, I promise,
and I don't want to see you cry.

Sarah Hirons (15)
Ashlawn School, Rugby

My Little Friend

His eyes are filled with elegance
His body as sleek as silk
His petite heart
Is as big as the treasure of the oceans
He has the speed of lightning
His muscles tensing to and fro
Just look at that little rocket go!
But now it's draining out
My little friend is getting frail
And pretty soon he'll fail
There is not much time

My little friend is my dog Sparky.

Richard Lines (15)
Ashlawn School, Rugby

Give Us A Reason

Give us a reason why we
Should spell it your way
When we can spell it
Our way!

Give us a reason why we have
To think your way
When we can think
Our way!

Give us a reason why we
Have to write your way
When we can write
Our way!

People say we're different
And we are different
And we stay different
Until different
Is all you can
Accept
Then we will be the
Same.

Michael Hollowell (15)
Ashlawn School, Rugby

Untitled

As the tree blows
And the wind flows
I watch and watch and watch
I watch the way she cooks and cleans
And the way she looks after us
I admire the way she works and works
And never lets me down
The way she let me do things
And never with a frown
And now I think and think and think
I now know how much she does
I'm now not to sit and twiddle my thumbs
I'm going to help my loving mum.

Will Headley (16)
Ashlawn School, Rugby

Does He

I've always wondered if he likes me or not
If he cares about me or not, but does he?
It seems as though he favours my brother
My brother is his genes, I was just added on when he met my mum.

I feel insecure about his feelings
As he never speaks them aloud,
I never ring him,
And when I see him it's for five minutes.

And when I do all it is is, 'Hi,'
With false smiles
And then he's off - without a goodbye.

I always thought, *I don't like him,*
But now he's gone I no longer feel at home.
I know I like him,
I know I love him,
Yet does he feel the same?
I feel insecure, as he once told me he didn't.

But now the table's turned, he's moved out,
I thought it would help, it might have brought us closer.
But no, we moved further apart, but once we had a conversation,
Just us two on MSN and that night I cried myself to sleep.

I love, like and listen to him, but does he do and feel the same?
He told me that night that he hates being strangers.

I agree, I hate it too, and he also told me,
He loves me, and that I was smart, sensible and beautiful.
That was what made me cry, I never expected the things he said.
That was what shocked me, he said, 'Let me take you out sometime,'
But what will happen then?

I always thought he didn't like me, he didn't love me,
But now I understand that he doesn't speak his feelings.
So I must wait until the time is right.

I will never let him be replaced, he means so much to me,
And to hear him tell me that he loves me means so much to me.
I love my dad, I want him to know this,
He needs to understand, I love him.

Eloise Barret (14)
Ashlawn School, Rugby

The Monster In The Wardrobe

Laying there in the darkness, I can see him sitting there.
His small beady eyes watching me, watching, waiting.
He's crouched in the corner,
I can see him which means
He can see me!
I can see his hair, his red frizzy hair.
I can see his long, pointy nose, I can see his mouth,
His huge mouth, smiling, staring, sniggering, laughing loudly.
I know he's not there, but he is!
I know he's watching, waiting, like a cat before it pounces!
I reach for the light, *bing!*

He's gone! Back into the wardrobe, I'm safe!
Till tomorrow night . . .

Emily Waugh (13)
Ashlawn School, Rugby

Bored In School

As I sit on my seat, listening
to the teacher going on and on,
waiting for the bell to go,
I think to myself what I should be doing
instead of being in school.
I wish there was no school,
so I would never get bored,
but there is school,
so until I'm 16
I will always be bored in school.
I would rather be playin' footy
with the lads
or chillin' with my mates
instead of being in this class,
bored out of my face,
Writing this poem!

Tarot Aplin (13)
Ashlawn School, Rugby

A Day In The Life Of Me

I wish I could live in my dreams
With the blue rivers and silky streams.
Where butterflies flutter and trees wave,
Instead of where I live, I'd rather live in a cave.
The streets are dark and alleys darker,
But when I turn on the light,
The boys fall down in laughter.
When I go to school they all bully me,
When I go out and about they all try to mug me.
When I return back home, all bloody and battered,
I just go upstairs to escape any more beatings.

Chris James (13)
Ashlawn School, Rugby

What's There

As you look far into the distance
You're most likely to see, touch or smell,
Trees with branches hanging like arms.
Foggy clouds, brushing against your face,
Like a strong and angry wind.
Leaves cracking every step you make,
Dead, old plants, scraping against your ankles.
Like people on the floor grabbing at them.
Shadows sway with the fog,
This is not a place you want to be.

The darkness is scary,
With all the noises in the background.
Such as owls hooting,
And the gate in the distance squeaking.
I step up to the house,
I sweep off the cobwebs,
I turn the handle and open the door,
I see a shadow,
And then . . .

Jenny Thrower-Menzies (12)
Ashlawn School, Rugby

The Forest

The thick, overgrown forest, dark and spooky,
With the damp moss growing up the thick tree trunk.
The brambles and mushrooms hiding beasts
Amongst the bushes in the mist.
Foxes and wolves, don't be surprised if a bear creeps up.
Look up and see birds and squirrels leaping about.
What's that, dark and screaming aloud, craving for something?
But wait, oh no, it's coming down . . .

Thomas Allman (12)
Ashlawn School, Rugby

Stamford Bridge - The Home Of The Chelsea Lions

On the train, so cramped, all you can see is blue, the Chelsea blue.
All you can hear is Chelsea, names, the legends, the goals.
Off the train, on the road, you can see street merchants
And burger vans.
All you can hear is Chelsea chants, so intimidating.

Approaching the bridge, Stamford Bridge, the road is so full,
So amazing to know that everyone here loves Chelsea.
Like me, so much blue, but so beautiful.
In the ground with my programme and drink,
Going to the front with my autograph book, hoping to get one.
An autograph.
The game, young and old alike watching the game with such
Concentration, waiting for a goal, yes, yes, we scored.
Wow, Joey Cole, now let me celebrate.

Thomas Wood (12)
Ashlawn School, Rugby

The Sea

The clear blue sea, yellow beach.
Looking out to sea I see the horizon.
It's all calm and peaceful.
There's a cool breeze in the air.
The sun's beating down at its hottest.
It cannot last forever.
The clear blue sea, yellow beach.
I can hear the ice cream van
A stampede of people,
Families, children, surfers, swimmers.
There is a fish,
Bucket and spade, ball, shell, surfboards on the beach.
The sun sets and people are going, leaving the sea.
The clear blue sea, yellow, sandy beaches.

Inderveer Uppal (12)
Ashlawn School, Rugby

Spain

Scorching, sweltering Spain
The salty smelling beaches.
The children screaming, the sun beaming,
And Spanish people getting suntanned.

The busy streets crawling with people,
The bright lights,
The restaurants smelling nice.
The nice, friendly atmosphere.
It makes me want to go back every year.

Amber Collings (12)
Ashlawn School, Rugby

Hallowe'en

One stormy night
Children were everywhere giving people a fright.
Two children went up the hill
To the castle, they never made their will.
The big door creaked open,
Bats and owls flew out of the door.
It smelt like dead people.
Of course there was more to come.
They walked into different rooms,
But everywhere was deserted.
There were no windows,
It was pitch-black.
The door slammed shut,
The children screamed
And there it ended.

Brodie Neville (12)
Ashlawn School, Rugby

Rain

The rain is coming back again,
It is very cold
And the men are quite bold,
There are so many bats
As well as rats.
It is always stormy,
And dirty and damp.
It's very dark so you may need a lamp.
This place is creepy,
It makes you sleepy,
All the roads are slippery,
As if you feel jittery.
We never get to see the sun,
But we can buy an iced bun.

Elizabeth MacLeod (12)
Ashlawn School, Rugby

Forest

The whistle of the trees, the squeal of the bats.
The shimmer of the sun, the mist of the night.
Hot to cold.
Light to dark.
Blackness of the forest.

The secret eyes are watching.
The sinking eye of predator on prey.
The creatures of the night come out for food.
The quiet of the bat, the howling of the wolf.
Blackness of the forest.

The birth of the forest.
Lightning to fire, wood to ash.
Death of green.
Seed and water.
The crack of life.
Rest, sweet forest.

Niall Neeson (12)
Ashlawn School, Rugby

Two Worlds

Where one side is warm the other is cold,
In the middle is a short winding road.
When you look to one side the sun is so bright,
And there are no people in sight,
With cactus swaying in the wind.

As the other is so cold the polar bears can't feel their toes.
Ice all over with some water at the side,
And penguins catching small fish with pointy noses.

So as you can see it's so different on either side,
But which one would you decide to go to?

Danielle Parker (12)
Ashlawn School, Rugby

The Place And The House

The house is all spooky
And the owls are watching everyone.
The place is lively and musty.
The house is echoing.
The place is dark and gruesome.
The house is always haunted.
The place is full of space.
The house is as scary as can be.

Arianna McKechnie (13)
Ashlawn School, Rugby

Sword City

As I walked into the City of Swords, this is what I saw . . .
I saw a graveyard that was the most hostile and superstitious place.
The scariest most ghostly, dusty, eerie, humungous place.
But the worst was still to come as I walked into this city.

As I left this city the most heavenly nice draught of air went past me,
It was a sweet wave,
As I went home!

Moneeb Razaq (12)
Ashlawn School, Rugby

Dark House

As I tiptoe through this terrible place
A look of shock upon my face.
Standing on creaking floorboards at slowest place,
I think this house is such a disgrace.

Chairs are damp,
Window sills are cold,
Surely this house is a hundred years old.

The rusty pipes in the bathroom they sit,
They must have not liked this house, not a single bit.

The ceiling is at its weakest point,
The plaster is cracked.
I should not have seen this joint,
The work here was lax.

The door knobs are crooked,
Rooms are eerie and dark.
The oven's not working,
Not a single spark.

I've found the light switch now,
It's not scary at all.
This house is just lovely,
With rooms for us all.

William Fulthorpe (12)
Ashlawn School, Rugby

The Sea

The sea is surrounding us,
The sea is bright as a moon,
The sea is bluer than the sky,
Quiet like puppies asleep,
Deserted as if no one was breathing,
The sea glitters in the sunlight.

When summer arrives, the sea is used,
Fun like a huge pool,
Crowded as a football match,
Loud as a classroom filled with chatty kids,
But still shining in the sunlight.

Summer's gone and winter's back,
The sea turns bright as the moon,
Turning blue as the summer's sky,
Deserted as if everyone's heart's stopped,
The sea glitters in the sunlight.

Becky Turtle (13)
Ashlawn School, Rugby

Some Day I Will Stand Up To You

On the way home from school,
dreading the time when I get to the park,
I drag my feet . . . slowly . . . slowly,
. . . the time has come . . .

You four boys are in a huddle,
waiting for the moment of delight,
picking . . . beating . . . on a scared wimpy mouse.
Oh, what shall I do?

After my time with you bullies,
I walk home, my head hurting and aching,
I tell no one, no one at all.
A small helpless bat.

But one day I shall stand up to you
and thrash you to the ground,
then I will be a person; not a lonely,
pathetic nobody.

Megan Ryan-Smith (11)
Ashlawn School, Rugby

The Battle
(Based on chapter four of 'Beowolf' entitled Grendel)

The smell of death prowled the moors,
The breeze whispered words of warning,
As endless blackness hunted the night sky
The hills that held secrets cast shadows.
The moon, that was darker than usual, cast glimpses
of the night stalker.
For terror would return to the village,
But tonight was different . . .

Pushing at least two metres every stride
The muscular, powerful figure over the hills did glide,
Until he met a large oak door,
Where his scale-ridged head sniffed and pursued,
The human flesh and the joy of the kills,
But tonight was different . . .

Green embers filled the doorway,
Fuelled with rage the creature came,
Seizing and tearing his naïve victims limb from limb.
Floods of scarlet showered the floor,
Once warm blood chilled as life trickled away,
But tonight was different . . .

A stroke of fear filled the creature,
A bitter taste, till now unknown.
Two powerful beings locked in turmoil.
What once was given was now received,
Terror, death and haunting.
What once was the predator was now the prey,
For tonight was different . . .

Sinews cracked and muscles ruptured,
Howls and bellows and cries of pain.
Reeling in battle, turmoil abound,
Pondering citizens gathered outside.
The hero's companions sprung to their feet,
Their swords bounced off the creature like rubber off metal,
Tonight was different . . .

Thunderous strength was summoned,
Both hero and creature broke free.
The creature's limbs ripped like paper,
For the hero's grasp bore victory.
As tonight was different.

Charles Whitehouse (11)
King Edward's School, Birmingham

Every Day I Got Bullied

Every day I got bullied,
I got angry and mad,
It does hurt my feelings,
It broke my heart.

I want it to stop,
It's never easy,
Stand in my shoes and feel my pain.

Naomi Faria (15)
Round Oak School, Leamington Spa

Birth Of An Island

The sea heaves,
Waves, like titanic serpents
Twist and hiss.

Monstrous contractions
Swell the belly of the ocean.

The waters break with a gargantuan roar,
And the newborn emerges,
Fresh-faced, pure and ready
To take its place in the universe.

Dale Austin (13)
Round Oak School, Leamington Spa